RADICAL WORSHIP
FAMILY DEVOTIONAL

Email: *info@chosenstones.org*
Web address: www.chosenstones.org
Phone: (513) 779-2822
Write to:
 6229 Fairwind Dr.
West Chester, OH 45069

Chosen Stone Ministries
Alicia White

Radical Worship Family Devotional
Second Addition Copyright © 2017 by Alicia White
Published by Chosen Stones Ministries
Email: info@ChosenStones.org
Web: www.chosenstones.org
Call: 513-779-2822

All illustrations and photos are copyrighted under Chosen Stones Ministries. Without written consent no illustrations or photos may be reproduced or copied for any reason.

Unless noted, all scripture is from the New King James Version of the Holy Bible

No part of this book, in any form (electronic, mechanical, photocopying or recording) may be reproduced unless written consent is given in advance by the author.

Table of Contents

About Our Ministry..4

Radical Worship family Devotional Vision..................6

How to Use this Devotional......................................8

What is Worship?..9

Why We Worship...15

Worship Changes Your Spirit..................................21

Worship Changes your Soul and Flesh....................37

Tabernacle in Us...33

Shadows of the Trinity...39

The Altar of Sacrifice...45

The Bronze Laver..51

The Lampstand...57

The Table of Showbread..63

The Altar of Incense..69

The Ark of the Covenant..75

Radical Worship..81

About Our Ministry

Chosen Stones Ministries

Chosen Stones Ministries is a focused spirit lead and spirit empowered ministry to families; teaching families how to live and walk by the spirit of God and how to worship in spirit and in truth making worship a lifestyle not a place they go.

We host monthly presence-driven family worship gatherings that engage all ages of the family young and old alike. In these gatherings we train families how to worship together and make a habituation place for the Holy Spirit through modeling and facilitating what we call "acts of Worship". These acts of worship often time use object lessons like communion, laying on of hands, studying and discussing scripture, praying scripture, listening for the voice of God, and using the gifts of the Spirit, all within the paradigm of the family.

It is our desire that the church at large grab hold of our vision for families and begin to host their own presence-driven family worship gatherings. As we equip the families of God to live a lifestyle of worship and create an altar for His presence within their home, our churches will become stronger, more spiritually mature, and filled with the presence of God. It starts in the home!

I currently write presence driven family devotionals for families, host yearly training conferences that include parents, and accept invitations to come to churches to train leaders and parents, and host family conferences.

Alicia White, founder and Director of Chosen Stones Ministries

www.chosenstones.org, more information: info@chosenstones.org

Kids in Ministry international Ohio

Kids in Ministry International Ohio is a sister ministry to Kids in Ministry int., founded and directed by Becky Fischer in North Dakota. We carry Becky's heart and vision here in Ohio to take the children of God beyond the limitations of man and allow the Holy Spirit, which has no limitations of age, to take over their lives. Far too many years we have held the umbrella of expectation too low for our children in the body, the result being boredom and a mass exodus of children leaving the church when they turn 18 never to return again. It is time that our children experience authentic relationship with Jesus through a spirit-driven life and heavenly supernatural invasions that empower them to do the work of ministry in these last days.

Children can and will experience the tangible presence of God and receive and use the gifts of the Holy Spirit if we allow them opportunity to do so. "Church as usual" will not satisfy this supernatural reality TV generation of the present age. God is pouring down the promise of the Father, "and it shall come to pass in the last days, says God, that I will pour out my spirit on all flesh; your sons and your daughters shall prophesy" (Acts 2:17, NKJV).

At KIMIOhio It is our purpose to train children's leaders how to step out of the box of religion and tradition and embrace teaching children the meat of God's word, activate them in the gifts, and bring them into an encounter with the presence of God on a weekly bases in our churches. We host annual training conferences, revival services, and kid and family conferences. We offer the *School of the Supernatural* and *PowerClub* training for leaders and parents, and many curriculum resources for children's leaders to use to help them facilitate this vision in their ministry. We also accept invites to come host an event in churches of Ohio.

Alicia White, Ohio Director of Kids in Ministry International Ohio

www.kimiohio.org, more information: kimiohio@ymail.org

Radical Worship Family Devotional Vision

What is Radical?

When you say the word radical you equate that with an extreme difference of what is traditionally the case. Although this is a true definition of radical it is also coupled with a definition that says to form a bases, foundation, and going to the root of something. In the case of this Radical Worship Family Devotional, both of those definitions encapsulate what this devotional is all about.

What is Worship?

Today worship is widely been defined by the two fast songs and one slow song we sing in our adult and children congregations. It has become a place we go and not a lifestyle we live. However, this is not a biblical definition of what true worship is all about. Worship in its simplest definition is one's heart, body, soul, and spirit given over to God for Him to do as He pleases. Worship is not to be defined by the songs we sing or the music we play, or even the place we go, but instead a life lived in obedience and sacrifice through Christ, honoring Him as the giver of life and Lord of all, all the rest of what we call worship is simply as manifestation or act of the true worship within our heart. Worship was the very road God established to lead us into communion, fellowship, and presence of our heavenly Father. However, somewhere along the way we lost the heart of what worship is and why we worship to begin with. Recently George Barna put out statistics that said that 1/3 of adults who attend worship services on a weekly bases say they have never experienced the presence of God, 2/3 of them when asked to define worship had no idea, less than 1/2 of all of them said that they ranked worship as a priority of their life. The reality is worship has become a portion of a church program rather than a required way of living in order to become a holy dwelling place of the living God.

The result of the lack of understanding, desire, and engagement into a lifestyle of worship within the body of Christ has had many detrimental consequences. In general, many in the body of Christ have lost their respect, reverence, and honor for our holy and sovereign God; leading the way of a lack of obedience and the fear of the Lord.

What is the Father Seeking?

Have you ever wondered why Jesus said to the women at the well, ***"But the hour is coming, and now is, when the true worshipers will worship the Father in spirit and truth; for the Father is seeking such to worship Him" John 4:23 (NKJV)?*** Jesus didn't say that the Father was seeking out those who could heal the sick, those who could prophecy, and those who could preach or teach, although those things are pleasing to the Lord. But Jesus said that the Father was seeking worshipers, but not just any worships, but those who will worship in spirit and in truth. The heart of the Father in heaven cries out to tabernacle and dwell with His children, and worship in truth defined by God's word, and worship in Spirit defined by who God is, is the only way He can be with His children; that is me and you. God is beckoning a generation that will leave the comfortable place of tradition, religion, and complacency, and surrender all of themselves to a lifestyle of worship not defined by man but defined by God; that is radical worship.

A Radical Worshipping Generation

This family devotional is all about redefining for a generation, based upon the word of God, what true worship is, what true worship produces, and how to worship in spirit and in truth; creating a radical worshipping generation of families that has come back to the foundation and root of worship itself, and through their own radical worship they will change the environment of our churches, communities, and the world.

HOW TO USE THIS DEVOTIONAL

This Radical Worship Family Worship Devotional was written for families with children of all ages.

There are 52 days your family can experience learning about what worship is, what happens when we worship, and God's biblical order of worship together. They are broken out into 13 main subjects, with 3 days of lessons for each and one day set aside for experiencing the Radical Worship together. For each devotional there is a suggestion for discussion and three main questions to find out if your whole family has understood what they were just taught.

You can use this family worship devotional every day, following along the teachings for 52 straight days, you can use it once a week making it a full year devotional, or you can use it to fit your schedule completing it on your time line. However, in whatever way you choose, the teachings are meant to be received in order, so I would not recommend randomly picking a devotional to do for a given day.

The *"Experiencing Radical Worship"* section found on the fourth day of each subject devotional is meant to conclude and bring together the topic your family has been learning for the last three devotional times. This time is so important because it seals into your spirit what you have just absorbed with your minds. Leave enough time on this day to let the Holy Spirit do His work in each one of you as you worship together.

RADICAL WORSHIP
FAMILY DEVOTIONAL

"No servant can serve two masters; for either he will hate the one and love the other, or else he will be loyal to the one and despise the other. You cannot serve God and mammon." Luke 16:13

DAY 1

THE HEART OF WORSHIP

Can anyone tell me what worship is? Is it clapping your hands, singing, or raising your hands? We often define worship by the singing of songs in a corporate service, but that isn't the definition of worship, simply an expression or the evidence of true worship going on inside of you. You see true worship is a reverence, love, and devotion (obedience) to a higher being or object, what we do to express that love, devotion and obedience is what we call acts of worship or expressions of worship. Worship looks a little like this: your setting in a car you call your life, and in the driver seat is whatever you choose to worship; that is to love above everything else, honor above everything else, and obey above everything else. The object or deity that you worship could be Jesus, it could be money, or anything you were devoted to. No matter what it is, it will be the one thing that determines where you go and what you do in this journey called life. When you worship something or someone they hold your outermost love, respect, and devotion; meaning they hold the power to your life. Worship is an issue of the heart. Whatever/whomever you decide to worship will have your heart.

FAMILY DISCUSSION

Spend some time with your family acting out the above analogy by taking two chairs, one behind the other, and having each person sit in the seat behind the driver as you ask them who is driving the? Who or what determines where they go and what they do? Who/what has their heart?

1. What are things like raising our hands, singing, clapping called?
2. What is true worship?
3. What determines where we go and what we do in life?

Prayer: God help us give our whole heart over to you in worship; that we may love you more than we love anything else, that we may obey you above everything else, and that we may reverence you above all else. Amen.

THE PERVERSION OF WORSHIP

The original intent of worship was to express love, obedience, and reverence to God and God only. In heaven, before the earth was created, Satan was the head angel of worship in Heaven, according to theologians. As the head worshipper, Satan saw the power of worship and began to have thoughts of rebellion in His heart towards God. In Isaiah 14:13-14 Isaiah describes what was in Satan's heart, *"For you have said in your heart: 'I will ascend into heaven, I will exalt my throne above the stars of God; I will also sit on the mount of the congregation on the farthest sides of the north; ¹⁴ I will ascend above the heights of the clouds, I will be like the Most High" (NKJV).* Satan's rebellion against God introduced perverted and twisted worship away from its original intent. Now Satan also had his throne in which the angels of darkness (demons) worshipped him; he was in His own driver seat. When Satan came to Eve in the garden convincing her she could become like God if she ate from the tree of good and evil, they disobeyed God taking their heart from God and giving it to Satan; giving their worship, love, and devotion over to Satan. Satan obtained power over humanity through one act of perverted and twisted worship.

FAMILY DISCUSSION

Discuss with your family the similarities between Satan's heart's desire to be like God leading Him to disobedience and Eve's heart's desire to be like God leading her to disobedience. Wanting to be our own God, the one who has power over our own life, is how we pervert our worship away from God. Discuss ways as a family that you can or have done that.

1. Who was all the worship originally supposed to go to?
2. What is perverted worship to God?
3. How did Satan obtain power over humanity?

Prayer: God we see through Adam and Eve how easy it is to be tempted to give our heart of worship over to another. Please help us to always obey you and convict us when our heart begins to stray from you. Amen.

DAY 3

THE BATTLE FOR OUR HEART

God seeing what had happened in the garden was saddened for His children. He desired their worship back, not because He wanted power over humanity, but because He was their Father and jealous for their love and missed being with them. How would your natural father feel if He didn't have your love? So in Genesis 3:21 God Himself had Adam and Eve cover with the blood and skin of an animal. This was the very first picture we see in the scriptures of what would be required of us to give our heart back to God; receiving the flesh and blood of the Lamb of God we call Jesus. However, mankind continued to sin and was trapped in a battle between the Kingdom of Darkness and the Kingdom of Heaven. Sin left mankind slaves to Satan, allowing him to lead us in what we do, say, and think. The people of God tried to worship God, Satan, and even idols that other people made into gods. Jesus said, **"No servant can serve two masters; for either he will hate the one and love the other, or else he will be loyal to the one and despise the other. You cannot serve God and mammon" (Luke 16:13, NKJV).** You can't be in two seats at the same time; allowing you, God, and Satan to drive you in what you do and where you go in life.

FAMILY DISCUSSION

Discuss with your family perhaps times where you have seen a battle between the Kingdom of Darkness and the kingdom of Heaven in your own life. Perhaps a certain situation in school or at home where you wanted to do something but in your heart you knew it would not be obeying what God wants you to do.

1. What did the Act of Worship in the garden point to as a way to give God our Heart back?
2. What causes the battle between the two Kingdoms in our life?
3. What back seat are you in today? Who has your heart? Who is driving your life?

Prayer: God we declare you will stay in the driver seat of our family. Help us to always repent and come back to you when we sin. You are jealous for our love and heart because you are a loving Father, and we want to be your loving children. We will serve you and you alone. Amen.

RADICAL WORSHIP
FAMILY REVIEW

"No servant can serve two masters; for either he will hate the one and love the other, or else he will be loyal to the one and despise the other. You cannot serve God and mammon." Luke 16:13

DAY 4

The last three days of the devotional your family should have gained an understanding of what true worship is all about; a heart issue verses simply just something we sing. You have walked through the original birthing place of worship in heaven with an understanding that God's original intent of worship was to give our heart, love, and devotion to God and God alone. Satan's disobedient actions in heaven, however, perverted worship giving way to mankind's battle for their heart between the kingdom of Darkness and the kingdom of Heaven.

EXPERIENCING RADICAL WORSHIP:

For your family worship time today you are going to challenge your family to answer the question "What seat are they in; who or what do they give their worship to"? As your worship allow each person time to reflect on that question, addressing any family member that needs to take the first step of worship in giving their lives to Jesus. Then, end the worship time with a powerful activity. Lay a clay object that represents an idol on a sturdy chair and invite each member of your family to come and repent for worshipping a false idol (encourage them to name it), and then with a hammer have them hit the idol. This will be loud and messy so make sure to prepare ahead of time to ensure safety of the kids. End with a victory song.

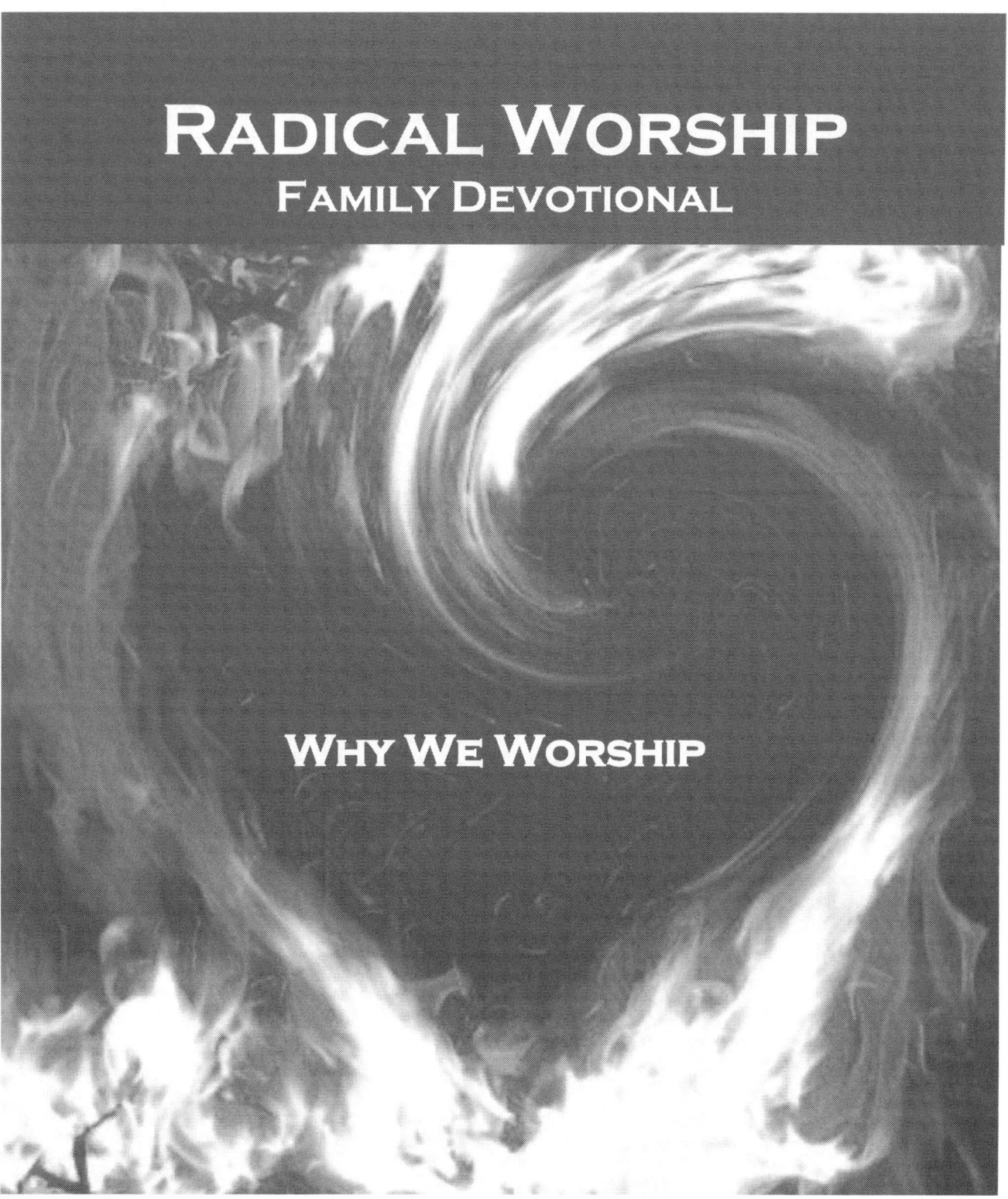

"But we all, with unveiled face, beholding as in a mirror the glory of the Lord, are being transformed into the same image from glory to glory, just as by the Spirit of the Lord." 2 Corinthians 3:18

Day 5

You Are Like a Chameleon Lizard

A Chameleon Lizard has the ability to change colors to look like whatever environment it is touching. If it is near leaf it becomes bright green, if it is on a branch it becomes brown. Did you know we have the ability to do that same thing? Who can say in here that they act like their sister mom, dad, brother sometimes? That is because you're around them the most and you begin to take on some of their characteristics. It is no different when it comes to our spiritual walk. God created man in His own image, and in the Garden, Adam and Eve where surrounded by the environment of heaven and had God's spirit living on the inside of them; they were constantly touching heaven. But when they sinned and were kicked out of the garden, God's spirit left them and they were left touching he world more than heaven. This changed how they thought and how they acted. They began to take on the characteristics of the world around them, and humanity no longer looked like God they looked like the world full of sin.

Family Discussion

Pull up a picture of a Chameleon Lizard from the internet and discuss with your family how it changes color with the environment it touches. Discuss some positive character traits that each family shares with each other. Than discuss what environments your family touches most and how it has effected what you look like.

1. What ability do we have that is like a Chameleon Lizard?
2. What caused humanity to start looking like the world?
3. What environment do you touch the most, heaven or the world?

Prayer: Jesus, you created us to have the ability to change our characteristics depending on what we touched. Your will was that we would always be touching heaven. Help our family to have more of heaven in our lives than anything else. Amen.

DAY 6

BEING BORN OF THE SPIRIT

You are made up of three parts, just like God has three parts. You have a flesh which is what we see on the outside. You have a soul which is what you feel and think. And you have a spirit which is dead before you're saved. Now before you receive Christ Ephesians 2:10 says, *"[you] were dead in trespasses and sins, ² in which [you] once walked according to the course of this world... fulfilling the desires of the flesh and of the mind..." (NKJV).* We are like walking dead people, zombies if you will before we are saved. However, when we received Jesus as our savior, our very first act of worship giving God back our heart, the Bible says were made alive or born again (John 3:3). Except this time, we were not born in flesh we were born in our spirit. It is as if we were standing in the Garden of Eden again and God breathed His life back into us. In fact, Jesus did this very thing to the disciples in John 20:22 as He breathed on them and said *"Receive the Holy Spirit"*. As the environment of God's presence and of heaven begin to touch us again, our spirits begin to change into the characteristic of Jesus.

FAMILY DISCUSSION

Pick three people in your family to me your flesh, soul, and spirit (label them with name tags). With them hooking arms allow the flesh and soul right behind lead the dead soul around like a walking zombie. Now, pretend that person was born again, have the spirit come alive. Discuss further with your family the idea of being born of the spirit and not of the flesh. Make sure everyone has had this experience, if not, lead them through salvation.

1. What are the three parts of you?
2. What part is dead before you are saved? What part leads you around?
3. What part of you is born again when you receive Jesus?

Prayer: Jesus, thank you for your spirit which has made us alive. Thank you that you have caused us to be born again. We are no longer zombies walking around dead in our sins lead by our flesh and soul. We now can touch heaven once again. Amen.

DAY 7

ONE DROP AT A TIME

The change in our spirits as we are born again doesn't happen overnight. It's like a cup of water and red food coloring. If I put one red drop of food coloring in a glass, what color will the water turn? Not quite red but an orangey color right? But what if I add many drops of red food coloring, the water will turn completely red right? Just like this water and food coloring, the more we touch heaven and are surrounded by the presence of God the more we change into the character of Christ and of heaven. How do we touch heaven? Every time we express are worship, our love, obedience, and reverence to God, the more God's presence comes down and dwells with us and changes us (James 4:8). But as it says in 2 Corinthians 3:18, the change is from glory to glory; one drop at a time. This is why worship is so important to God. When you were dead in your sins giving your heart over to Satan and worldly things you were being changed to look like the world. But as you begin to worship God you begin to receive the residue of Heaven instead.

FAMILY DISCUSSION

Demonstrate with your family the change that takes place with red food coloring and a glass of water. Allow the kids to help. Now discuss with them how that compares to our worship and the change in us.

1. Was there a difference in what the water looked like when you put one drop of food coloring in verses many drops?
2. What do we have to do to change more and more into the image of heaven and Christ?
3. Is the change all at once?

Prayer: Jesus may our house be filled with worship to you. As we lift you up, come and touch us with heaven, that we may be changed from glory to glory. We want to look like, act like, and sound like heaven and you Jesus. We want more drops of your blood in our life. Amen.

RADICAL WORSHIP
FAMILY REVIEW

"But we all, with unveiled face, beholding as in a mirror the glory of the Lord, are being transformed into the same image from glory to glory, just as by the Spirit of the Lord". 2 Corinthians 3:18 (NKJV)

DAY 8

The last three days of the devotional your family should have gained an understanding of why worship is so important. The fact is worship is the way that God has chosen not to just be with His children but to change His children into the image of His son. Your family should have gained an understanding of just how powerful worship is, no matter what you worship, and how one touch of heaven can begin to change a person into the image of Jesus.

EXPERIENCING RADICAL WORSHIP:

Your family worship time will focus on leading your family into worship that touches heaven. As you describe the description of heaven found in Revelation 1:12-16 and 4:2-8 have each family member beginning to draw what they hear. They will not be able to draw everything so just have them draw what stands out to them. Than as you begin to worship have each person stand, sit, or lay on their drawing imagining that they are touching heaven.

"If we live in the Spirit, let us also walk in the Spirit."
Galatians 5:25

DAY 9

WAIT FOR THE FULLNESS

Galatians 5:25 says, *"If we live in the Spirit, let us also walk in the Spirit" (Gal 5:25, NKJV).* God desires us to get to the point that our spirit, the person of the Holy Spirit within us, begins to lead us in our life. But as a babe in Christ, your spirit is still young, not having touched heaven enough to pull your flesh and soul the way of the spirit. However, the more you worship the more you change in to the characteristics of the person of the Holy Spirit who is living inside of you and your flesh and soul follow right in line. Acts 1:4 is a perfect example of this. Jesus had died and arose from heaven, and was about to ascend to be with the Father. He wanted them to go and spread the gospel in all the earth, but before they could be like Christ on earth, He told them to wait and worship in an upper room until the Holy Spirit came in His fullness. So as they worshiped in the upper room, day after day, they touched more and more of the environment of heaven, until the fullness of the spirit of God consumed their spirit (Acts 2:1-4).

FAMILY DISCUSSION

Discuss and demonstrate, using three family members again to be spirit, soul, and flesh, how your spirit is the very first thing that begins to change as you give God your heart in worship, but your flesh and soul are still the same and going in a different direction. Have them lock arms and create a tug-a-war. Now look up Acts 2:1-4 and discuss the story and what happened when the disciples worshiped over and over again in the upper room.

1. What part of our body does God desire to lead us?
2. Can our spirit lead us immediately after we are saved?
3. What must we do to become Christ on earth and to be led by our spirits?

Prayer: Jesus we ask now that you make our home an upper room experience. Give us the grace to worship and pray so more until the fullness of your spirit comes upon each one of us. We want to be led by the spirit of God, not our flesh or soul. Amen.

Eyes and Ears of Our Spirit

The first part of the scripture that describes what happened in the upper room says, *"And suddenly there came a sound from heaven, as of a rushing mighty wind" (Acts 2:2, NKJV).* They began to hear the sound of heaven the more they worshiped. Just like a baby, who before they are born hears only the heartbeat of their mother is suddenly introduced to a new environment and hears sounds never heard before, as we are born in the spirit we begin to hear sounds of our new environment heaven. This includes hearing the voice of God. How can we be led by God's spirit if we cannot hear His voice? The second thing we develop when the fullness of the spirit comes is we receive our spiritual eyes. *"Then there appeared to them divided tongues, as of fire, and one sat upon each of them" (Acts 2:3, NKJV).* When a baby is born they have very limited eyesight. The eyes are used to being in the dark, but the more time spent in the light of a new environment, the more the baby can see. So it is with us. Our eyes must adjust from living in the darkness of this world to the light of God's kingdom. The more we worship and touch heaven, the more we develop eyes to see in the spirit.

Family Discussion

As your bibles are open up to Acts 2:1-4, read together how the disciples received their spiritual eyes and ears on the day of Pentecost. For fun, blow up a balloon to represent your spirit and as you discuss draw ears and eyes on the balloon to begin to make it look like a person; the person of the holy Spirit. Take turns sharing the evidence in your own life of this happening.

1. What was the first thing that happened to the disciples on the day of Pentecost?
2. What was the second thing that happened to the disciples on the day of Pentecost?
3. Is their spirit's beginning to look like a person? Who would that person be?

Prayer: Jesus we pray now that you would give each one of us in this family eyes to see and ears to hear in the spirit. We pray that our spirits are consumed by the spirit of God, and we begin to hear your voice and see in heaven more than ever before. Amen.

DAY 11

THE LANGUAGE OF OUR SPIRIT

The third part of that scripture tells us what happens next in our spirits as we begin to worship and touch heaven. ***"And they were all filled with the Holy Spirit and began to speak with other tongues, as the Spirit gave them utterance." (Acts 2:4, NKJV).*** As they worshipped and touched heaven, they received their spiritual mouth to speak by the spirit. Just like a baby, who cannot speak at all when born, learns to speak the language of the new environment, so do we. The more we worship and touch heaven the more we develop in our spirits the mouth of the person of the Holy Spirit. We begin to speak what the spirit of the Lord is saying, otherwise known as the evidence of the baptism of the Holy Spirit. Your heavenly language, or spirit language, is simply an outward expression of this power and fullness of the spirit inside of you. There are basically two different types of languages you can get; known and unknown tongues. Known tongues is what the disciples had that day as they spoke in the native language of people around them without having learned that language. Unknown tongues is a language that is not understood by man but only by the person of the Holy Spirit. This prayer language as it is spoken makes your spirit strong enough to lead you.

FAMILY DISCUSSION

Go to Mark 16:17 as you discuss how Jesus said it would be a sign of a believer. Add a mouth to your balloon you used in the prior lesson. If one or several members of the family have received their language have them demonstrate it during the prayer time.

1. What was the third thing that happened to the disciples at Pentecost?
2. Who is speaking through us when we speak in our spirit language?
3. What happens when we begin to prayer in our spirit language?

Prayer: Dear Holy Spirit, come and baptize us with your language. Speak through us that we may build up muscles in our spirit. May our family carry this sign as believers in Christ and may it be just as normal for us to speak in our spirit language as our natural language. Amen.

RADICAL WORSHIP
FAMILY REVIEW

"If we live in the Spirit, let us also walk in the Spirit"
Galatians 5:25 (NKJV)

DAY 12

The last three days of the devotional your family should have gained an understanding of how the change in us starts in our spirit. You should have a new understanding of what happened on the day of Pentecost as the disciples received their spirit eyes, ears, and mouth. This is exactly the process that happens to us as we worship and touch heaven. Your family should be well prepared to receive the baptism of the Holy Spirit today in worship and begin to look like the person of the Holy Spirit.

EXPERIENCING RADICAL WORSHIP:

Your family worship time today will focus on the upper room experience. Set up the scene and encourage your family that you are going to do what the disciples were instructed to do by Jesus; wait and worship. As you begin to worship encourage them to take the picture they drew last week and lay, sit, or stand on it imagining that they are touching heaven. As you begin to go deep into worship encourage your family to begin to listen in the spirit, see in the spirit, and lastly lead them into praying in the spirit. Lay hands and pray for anyone who wants to receive their heavenly language.

"I have been crucified with Christ; it is no longer I who live, but Christ lives in me; and the life which I now live in the flesh I live by faith in the Son of God, who loved me and gave Himself for me." Galatians 2:20

DAY 13

THE FILTER OF OUR THOUGHTS

As we continue to give God our heart through worship, touching heaven and allowing our spirits to be changed, our spirits become a filter for the rest of our body. If we allow our spirit to lead us, everything that comes at us in life will go through our spirit first filtering out what is of God and what is not, thus changing what we think, feel, and do based upon our spirit. Our soul, what we think and feel, is a very powerful part of us. In fact, it only took one thought to create sin for all of humanity in the Garden of Eden. The question becomes what do we do with the thoughts that we have? The bible tells us that we are to **"have the mind of Christ" (1 Corinthians 2:16, NKJV).** So how do we get rid of the thoughts that are not Christ thoughts, by allowing our spirits to become a filter for our mind. Ephesians 4:22-23 says that we are to **"put off, concerning your former conduct, the old man which grows corrupt according to the deceitful lusts, [23] and be renewed in the spirit of your mind" (NKJV).** Just like water is renewed by a filter, we are to be renewed by our spirits. Our emotions, the other part of our soul, most always is directly related to the thoughts we are thinking; if we get our thoughts right our emotions will be right too.

FAMILY DISCUSSION

If you have a water filter demonstrate with your family what it does and compare it to the filer of our spirit and what it does. Discuss different thoughts that we all have and ask family members to tell you if they are of God or not. Discuss any situations that have come up lately that caused a person to have to renew their mind.

1. What is the filter for the rest of our body?
2. What does the filter of our spirit do?
3. What two things make up our soul?

Prayer: Dear God, help us to use the filter of our spirit with every thought that enters into our mind. I declare that our family will have the mind of Christ, putting off every thought that is not of you. Convict us God when we begin to entertain thoughts that are not of you. Amen.

WORSHIP CHANGES YOUR SOUL

The best example of how this worship process happens to change our thoughts and emotions is through the story of Jesus in the Garden (Matthew 26:36-46). Jesus knew His time was at hand to be crucified and in the garden we see Jesus struggle with sorrowful thoughts. However, Jesus decided to worship God anyways. Jesus told the disciples that He was going to pray and asked them to pray with Him. Immediately through Jesus' worship in prayer we can begin to see the change in His mind, but it took more than one moment of worship. In fact it took three times of worshiping God, touching heaven, and allowing His spirit to be a filter to bring complete change. 2 Corinthians 10:4-6 says, **For the weapons of our warfare are not carnal but mighty in God for pulling down strongholds, [5] casting down arguments and every high thing that exalts itself against the knowledge of God, bringing every thought into captivity to the obedience of Christ, [6] and being ready to punish all disobedience when your obedience is fulfilled" (NKJV).** Our greatest battle with the enemy is in our mind and our greatest weapon is our worship.

FAMILY DISCUSSION

As a family read the story of Matthew 26:36-46. Discuss the process Jesus went through in prayer to finally get to the place that His thoughts lined up with God's thought and he was ready to face the cross set before Him. Think of any situations within your family that worshipping could have helped or did help you change your mind and emotions about something.

1. How was Jesus' soul feeling as He thought about going to the cross?
2. What helped Him change His mind and prepare Him to do God's will?
3. How many times of worshipping did it take Jesus before He changed His mind?

Prayer: God, if Jesus struggled with thoughts and feelings that were not of you, I know we will too. Help us to react to ungodly thoughts and emotions like Jesus; help us to choose to worship you anyways. Our worship is our weapon; give us the grace to use it. Amen.

WORSHIP CHANGES YOUR FLESH

Romans 13:14 says, *"put on the Lord Jesus Christ, and make no provision for the flesh, to fulfill its lusts" (NKJV).* We are to do, say, and go as Christ did these things. Once again we turn our attention to the garden with Jesus to see how worship affects our flesh. The will of the Father for Him was to be crucified, but in that garden Jesus was struggling with fulfilling the lust of His flesh, which was to not experience any pain or death at the hands of the people. But the third time He worshiped through prayer His spirit had strengthened and Jesus stood up and was willing to go; His soul and flesh submitted and changed their directions. As Jesus physically went and was willing to crucify His flesh, Jesus asked us to do the same; *"take up the cross, and follow Me" (Mark 10:21, NKJV).* Jesus isn't saying that we, our flesh, must literally die on a cross, but He is saying that we must be willing to go, say, and do as Jesus has done. Peter said this about His life, *"I have been crucified with Christ; it is no longer I who live, but Christ lives in me" (Galatians 2:20, NKJV).* Peter was willing to die to his own desires and instead allowed Christ to take over His very flesh. He lived a lifestyle of worship to Jesus, and so should we.

FAMILY DISCUSSION

As a family review the story of Matthew 26:36-46. Discuss about how Jesus' emotions and thoughts affected what His flesh wanted to do. Discuss situation your family has had that affected what your flesh wanted to do and discuss how worship did or would of affected the outcome.

1. How did Jesus' thoughts affect His flesh?
2. What was the will of God for Jesus' flesh?
3. What is the will of God for our flesh?

Prayer: Jesus, help each of one us pick up our cross and follow you. Use our worship to kill our own desires and flesh that you may live through us. May every place we go and everything we do be as you would go and do. Amen.

RADICAL WORSHIP
FAMILY REVIEW

"I have been crucified with Christ; it is no longer I who live, but Christ lives in me; and the life which I now live in the flesh I live by faith in the Son of God, who loved me and gave Himself for me.

Gal 2:20 (NKJV)

DAY 16

The last three days your family should have gained an understanding of the change that goes on inside of our soul and flesh as we worship, touch heaven, and our spirit becomes a filter that brings change and begins to lead our life. Jesus' struggle in the garden is a beautiful picture of how we all struggle with thoughts, emotions, and lust of the flesh, and what He did with those ungodly thoughts and emotions is an example for us all on how we are to live; a lifestyle of worship.

EXPERIENCING RADICAL WORSHIP:

Your family worship time today will focus on encouraging your family to worship, allowing their spirits to become a filter for their soul and flesh. With each of them having a blank piece of paper, have them write down some ungodly thought they have had this week. As you begin to go deeper into worship, encouraging them to touch heaven, have them ask Jesus to help them remove their ungodly thoughts and replace them with His. Also, have them ask Jesus to reveal any other thoughts they may have that isn't of Him. As they are going through this process have them on a new sheet of paper, write down any new thoughts they receive. End this time by asking the family to focus on anything that Jesus might be asking them to do, go, or say, surrendering themselves to a lifestyle of obedience and worship.

"Do you not know that you are the temple of God and that the Spirit of God dwells in you?" 1 Corinthians 3:16

Day 17

The First Tabernacle on Earth

A tabernacle is a place that you go to worship and be with God; a holy place that holds the presence of God. We call it a church, temple, or a sanctuary. When God created Adam and Eve in His image He desired to have a place where He could come and dwell and be with His children. God was holy and perfect, as well as Adam and Eve, and this holiness demanded a holy environment to dwell in. The Garden of Eden was created to be a copy of heaven, God's original holy home. God created within the garden a river of life, the tree of life, and the tree of good and evil which were things that were original to heaven as it says in Revelation 22:2. God designed a holy place, or tabernacle, on earth so that He Himself could come and feel at home. We know that God walked and talked with Adam and Eve in this original holy tabernacle according to the scripture in Genesis 3:8-9. However, that did not last for long. Adam and Eve were kicked out of the Garden of Eden, God's original holy tabernacle, because they disobeyed God and fell into the temptation of Satan by eating of the tree of good and evil; no longer where they holy as God was holy. Because of this, God had to ban them from the garden, never to return (Genesis 3:22-24).

Family Discussion

Revisit the story of Adam and Eve and the Garden of Eden (Genesis 1:26-3:1-12). As you read the scriptures that describe the garden compare them with Revelation 22:2 describing heaven. Discuss with your family how the place God created on earth to be with His children was the very first tabernacle on earth.

1. What is a tabernacle?
2. Why was the Garden of Eden created?
3. Why did Adam and Eve have to leave the first tabernacle on earth?

Prayer: God from the very beginning of the creation of earth your heart has always been turned towards being with your children. Help us to have eyes to see and ears to hear what you are saying. Amen.

Day 18

Tabernacle Made from Man

God missed being with His people. He was not just a God, but a father and fathers desire to be with their children. Because God is Holy, His holiness prevented Him from coming near His children or even looking at them as it says in Habakkuk 1:13. So God designed a plan to create the second tabernacle on earth. God gave Moses blueprints from heaven in exodus 25:8 to build a tabernacle to hold His presence so He could come down and dwell with His people again. God, like He did with the Garden of Eden, designed a holy place that would look like His home according to Hebrews 8:5. The Tabernacle was divided into three parts: the outer court, the inner court (Sanctuary), and the holiest of all (the most holy place). Within these three sections God strategically placed the furniture pieces which all had a specific purpose. Within the outer court, the altar of burnt offerings or altar of sacrifice, as it is also called, and the bronze laver were placed. Within the inner court or sanctuary, the lampstand, the table of showbread, and the altar of incense were placed. Within the most holy place, the Ark of the Covenant was placed. All together, these areas made up the tabernacle of Moses. This tabernacle was made of cloth and was portable so it could move with the children of Israel as they traveled in the wilderness.

Family Discussion

Take some time to look up and read the scriptures with your family discussing how God's heart was constantly turned towards building a tabernacle on earth so He could be with His children.

1. What was the second tabernacle on earth called?
2. What was it a copy of?
3. What was the three parts of the tabernacle?

Prayer: God once again we see your heart to build a tabernacle on this earth so that you may dwell with your people. Your desire to be with us is revealed in your word. Help us gain an understanding for your heart as a father. Amen.

Tabernacle Made of Flesh

The Tabernacle of Moses was only to be a foreshadow of the third and final one yet to come on earth. Foreshadowing is to give a clue of things to come in the future. Paul speaks of this type of foreshadowing in Colossians 2:17 when he talks to the church about all the rituals, traditions, laws, and festivals of the Old Testament are shadows of things to come in Christ. It is the same principle as a shadow of a person on a wall. The shadow is not the real thing, but a clue as to what the real thing looks like. 1 Corinthians 3:16 says, ***Do you not know that you are the temple of God and that the Spirit of God dwells in you" (NKJV).*** When God created the Tabernacle of Moses in the wilderness, He knew in the back of His mind that one day the place of His tabernacle would become you and me. We are to be the very place God comes down and dwells; the very holy place of worship. From the outer court where the altar of sacrifice is to the most holy place where the Ark of the Covenant is placed, it is all in us. Remember too, that the tabernacle is a copy of the Kingdom of Heaven where God lives. Jesus says in Luke 17:21, ***"For indeed, the kingdom of God is within you" (NKJV).*** As we become the tabernacle of God, the kingdom of Heaven is represented in us.

Family Discussion

Take the time again to look up the scriptures with your family, discussing God's thoughts and plans to make us the ultimate tabernacle. Ask each one how it makes them feel to imagine that you were created to look like heaven.

1. What does foreshadow mean?
2. What is the third and final tabernacle on earth?
3. What three places dwell inside of you just as they do in the tabernacle of Moses?

Prayer: God how awesome our ways and majestic our your thought towards us that you would desire to dwell in man above all else. May this family be your tabernacle, individually and together. May we always be a copy of heaven on earth. Amen.

RADICAL WORSHIP
FAMILY REVIEW

"I have been crucified with Christ; it is no longer I who live, but Christ lives in me; and the life which I now live in the flesh I live by faith in the Son of God, who loved me and gave Himself for me.

Gal 2:20 (NKJV)

DAY 20

The last three days your family should have gained an understanding as to what a tabernacle is and the progression of the tabernacles on the earth ending with us being the ultimate tabernacle of God. This lessons sets the scene for study the tabernacle of Moses as a foreshadow of us as the tabernacle made of flesh.

EXPERIENCING RADICAL WORSHIP:

Today's family worship time will focus the families' attention on how they are to become the very place of worship, the tabernacle of God. Encourage them to realize they don't have to go to church to get into God's presence; they just have to desire to become God's tabernacle. As you worship today allow the Holy Spirit to begin to give them a reality of the tabernacle of the living God inside of them.

Radical Worship
Family Devotional

Shadows of the Trinity

"...The copy and shadow of the heavenly things."
Hebrew 8:5

DAY 21

THE SHADOW OF THE OUTER COURT

The tabernacle of Moses consisted of three major areas; the outer court, the inner court or sanctuary, and inner most court or the most holy. God also has three parts to Him; Father, Son, and Holy Spirit. So, we can begin to see that the tabernacle was actually a shadow of God Himself, each section representing a part of the trinity of God. Remember too, that the tabernacle is actually in you and me today. Do we have three parts to us? Yes as we have learned previously. The outer court was sectioned off by a cloth fence. This area was completely uncovered and was lit by the natural light of the sun. This was the foreshadow of God's son (sun) that was to be the light of the world according to John 8:12. Often, Jesus referred to us as sheep and He as the shepherd. If you look at the outer court, it could be recognized as a fenced in pasture for sheep. There was a gate or a door on the east side of the court and in John 10:9 Jesus is referred to as the door where we find pasture. Some people try to get close to God by climbing or jumping over the door or gate, but John 10:1 says we are considered thieves if we try to skip over Jesus in the Outer Court of our worship. There are no shortcuts to Gods presence; you must go through the door of Jesus. I also want to point out that this outer court represents your flesh, as Jesus came as God in the flesh.

FAMILY DISCUSSION

Take time with your family to look up the scriptures mentioned and discuss and compare them to the outer court of the tabernacle. It might be helpful if you find a picture of the outer court on the internet to get a clearer picture of what it looked like.

1. What 3 things were mentioned in this devotion that has three parts?
2. How is the outer Court lit with light and who does it represent?
3. What does the cloth fence of the outer court represent?

Prayer: God thank you for showing us so clearly the mysteries and shadows of the Outer Court of the tabernacle. Help us to have eyes to see the foreshadows revealed and how they connect to our worship. We desire your order of worship is this family and it starts with Jesus. Amen.

Day 22

The Shadow of the Inner Court

The inner court was covered under a large tent that actually held both the inner court and inner most court of the tabernacle which was divided by a large veil. The first thing you notice when you walk into this room is that it no longer is lit by the sun. Instead the inner court is lit by seven oil lamps on the lampstand. Oil was constantly maintained in the lamps in order to keep this room lit. The oil was their source of power just like electricity is for us. The oil represents the power and presence of His Holy Spirit. Often times oil was used to anoint people with the Holy Spirit (1 Samuel 16:13). So this room is obviously the Holy Spirit of the trinity of God. As the tabernacle of God what part does it represent in us? Psalms 23:5 says, *"You anoint my head with oil; My cup runs over" (NKJV).* What do we call the part of us that involves what we think or feel? It is our soul. This part of the tabernacle, the inner court, represents doing the work and ministry of the Holy Spirit. As Jesus commands us to go into all the world and make disciples, this is the step of our worship where that happens. The Holy Spirit works through our thoughts and our feelings to help us do God's work on earth.

Family Discussion

Take time with your family to look up the scriptures mentioned and discuss and compare them to the Inner court of the tabernacle. It might be helpful if you find a picture of the Inner court on the internet to get a clearer picture of what it looked like.

1. What was the Inner Court lit by?
2. What does the Oil represent in the Lamps?
3. What part of us does the Inner Court represent?

Prayer: God thank you for showing us so clearly the mysteries and shadows of the Inner Court of the tabernacle. Help us to have eyes to see the foreshadows revealed and how they connect to our worship. We desire your order of worship so we must be about our Father's business. Amen.

DAY 23

THE SHADOW OF THE MOST HOLY PLACE

In the Most Holy Place the Ark of the Covenant is the only furniture piece. The Ark of the Covenant was the very place God was thought to dwell in the Old Testament (Exodus 25:22). This room than obviously represents the Father of the trinity. This room was completely blocked from the outside world and its only means of light was the glory of God Himself. Isaiah 60:19 speaks of this glory light,
What does the shadow of inner most court represent in us? It represents our Spirit. The bible says in John 4:24 **"God is Spirit" (NKJV).** When God breathed into Adam he became a spirit being (Genesis 2:7). The word **breath** in that scripture means spirit. God breathed spirit into man. When Adam and Eve died however, their home for God within themselves died; their spirits died. They no longer could be the home of a Holy God. However, when Jesus came and died on the cross in place of us, all that changed. Jesus, after He died and before He went to heaven, did what he saw His father do in the Garden of Eden, **"He breathed on them, and said to them, "Receive the Holy Spirit" (John 20:22, NKJV).** The same happens to us when we receive Jesus as the Lamb of God. God, by His Holy Spirit comes into the ark of our tabernacle within our spirit.

FAMILY DISCUSSION

Take time with your family to look up the scriptures mentioned and discuss and compare them to the Most Holy place of the tabernacle. It might be helpful if you find a picture of the Most Holy place on the internet to get a clearer picture of what it looked like.

1. What furniture piece was in the Most Holy Place?
2. Who did the Most Holy place represent in the trinity of God?
3. What does the Most Holy place represent in us?

Prayer: God thank you for showing us so clearly the mysteries and shadows of the Most Holy place of the tabernacle. Help us to have eyes to see the foreshadows revealed and how they connect to our worship. We desire your order of worship that leads us right into your holy presence. Amen.

RADICAL WORSHIP
FAMILY REVIEW

"...The copy and shadow of the heavenly things"
Hebrew 8:5 (NKJV)

DAY 24

The last three days your family should have gained an understanding of the larger perspective of the Tabernacle of Moses; seeing the shadows and foreshadows of things to come, as well as, the overall picture of God's order of worship. Your family should have an understanding and conviction that there are no shortcuts to God's presence. If they want to be in God's presence, they must go through a specific process. By simply looking at the layout of the three parts of the tabernacle, your family should begin to see a shadow of the three parts of the Trinity of God as well as the three parts of us as the tabernacle of today.

EXPERIENCING RADICAL WORSHIP:

This worship experience will be a time to focus the family's attention on God's order or God's steps to arrive in His presence. Lay hands on each one of your family members, praying they go through the gate of Jesus, through the inner court; the work of the Holy Spirit, and they enter into the rest of the Lord where His presence abides. Worship the Lord together.

RADICAL WORSHIP
FAMILY DEVOTIONAL

THE ALTAR OF SACRIFICE

"But now in Christ Jesus you who once were far off have been brought near by the blood of Christ." Ephesians 2:13

DAY 25

A SACRIFICE REQUIRED

The Altar of Burnt Offerings, or the Altar of Sacrifice as it is called, is the very first furniture piece you see in the Outer Court. When God found Adam and Eve He covered them with animal skin. God needed a way for Adam and Eve's sin to be covered so God could come near them again. In Hebrews 9:22 the bible says. *"According to the law almost all things are purified with blood, and without shedding of blood there is no remission of sin" (NKJV).* If God was going to be able to enjoy being with His children, they would have to be cleansed and purified in blood. The bible also says in Romans 6:23, *"For the wages of sin is death" (NKJV).* There was a price to be paid for their sin, and that was death. God loved His children so He established an exchange offering; the animal's death for their life. When God established the Tabernacle of Moses to be the place where He would dwell and be with His children, the very first step was to cover their sins with the blood of animals and to reconcile the judgment of God for sin through the death of an animal. They would take a lamb, tie it across the altar, and then they would kill it. Without this step of worship no man could come close to God.

FAMILY DISCUSSION

Look up a picture of the Altar of Sacrifice from the internet. Discuss how necessary this step of worship was to be with a Holy God. God is a just God, there for this was justice for His law of sin.

1. What is the first furniture piece of the Outer Court?
2. What happens at this Altar of Sacrifice?
3. Why did blood have to be shed? Why did death have to occur?

Prayer: God thank you for making a way to be with your children. Your love for us is so deep that you choose to allow us to live despite our sin. Let the weight of our sin never leave our mind that we may understand that it takes blood and death to forgive us. Amen

DAY 26

A SHADOW OF CHRIST REVEALED

Jesus is not just the Son of God who died on the cross, He is the Lamb of God who shed His blood and died so we didn't have to (John 1:29). The Altar of Sacrifice was a foreshadow of Christ. The stone altar was simply replaced by a wooden tree in the New Testament. When God ordered the first step of worship in the tabernacle to be at the Altar of Sacrifice, He was simply setting up the scene for our very first act of worship; receiving Jesus as the Lamb of God who takes away our sin and death. Jesus exchanges His life for ours (Colossians 1:21-22). In Hebrews 10:4 it says, *"For it is not possible that the blood of bulls and goats could take away sins" (NKJV).* The blood of animals only covered the sin. They had to make a new sacrifice year after year. The blood of animals did not have the power to change the hearts of man, so they would not sin again, but the blood of Jesus, along with the Holy Spirit, has the power to remove sin completely. We are brought back into that holy image of God again through the blood and flesh of Jesus. Through Jesus, *"you who once were far off have been brought near by the blood of Christ" (Ephesians 2:13 (NKJV).*

FAMILY DISCUSSION

Pull up a picture of Jesus on the cross from the internet as you discuss and look up the above scriptures. Make sure your family has a clear picture of Jesus as the Lamb of God and why He had to die and shed His blood.

1. What was Jesus called at the Altar?
2. Why did Jesus have to die?
3. What is our very first act of worship?

Prayer: Jesus, thank you for being our Lamb of God who died and shed His blood so we could be brought near God once again. You died so we didn't have to...thank you. We recognize you as the Lamb of God and ask that you never let us forget what you did. Help us to always approach God through your sacrifice. Amen.

DAY 27

THE ALTAR IN US

The foreshadowing of the Altar of Sacrifice does not stop with Jesus. Remember, every furniture piece of the Tabernacle of Moses is now in us. We carry the Altar of Sacrifice within us as well. This altar in us represents the death and sacrifice of our flesh as we live through Christ. Jesus said in Luke 9:23 that we must deny ourselves and take up our own cross (altar). Receiving Jesus' death as the Lamb of God ensures us live eternal, but the second most important act of worship you could ever give to God is to lay *yourself* down on the Altar of Sacrifice and surrender your life, your desires, your will, and heart to Jesus. We are to become living sacrifice (Romans 12:1). In 1 Corinthians 15:31, Paul says he dies daily with Christ. That means, as we wake up every morning, we must decide if we are going to exchange what we want to do or think for what Christ wants to do through us. This is the act of making Jesus not just our savior but our Lord. To make Jesus Lord over your life is to make Him owner of your life. Your life is not your own, it is only through Christ that we can draw near to God. Galatians 2:20 says it like this, *"I have been crucified with Christ; it is no longer I who live, but Christ lives in me" (Gal 2:20, NKJV).*

FAMILY DISCUSSION

Take time to look up and discuss with your family the above scriptures mentioned. Discuss what it means to each one of you to take up your cross (altar) and follow Christ. How do you demonstrate acts of worship to God through being the living sacrifice?

1. What does the Altar of Sacrifice in us represent?
2. What does it mean to become a living sacrifice?
3. What does it mean to make Jesus Lord over our life?

Prayer: I declare that each member of this family will become a living sacrifice for you Jesus. What you want for us, where you want us to go, do, and say, is what we will do. Help us to die on our altar every day that Christ may live through us. Amen.

RADICAL WORSHIP
FAMILY REVIEW

"But now in Christ Jesus you who once were far off have been brought near by the blood of Christ."

Ephesians 2:13 (NKJV)

DAY 28

Your family should have the understanding through the last three lessons the reason why God chose the Altar of Sacrifice as the very first furniture piece. The reason being, God needed a way to make His children holy so that He could dwell in their presence. The Altar of Sacrifice was where animals were slaughtered as a required sacrifice. The blood and death of an animal was God's temporary requirement for the remission of man's sin. Your family should be able to recognize and see that this principle established at the tabernacle is the foreshadow of Christ as the Lamb of God who took away our sins once a for all. You family should also be able to see the shadow of us who are to live our lives as a living sacrifice through Christ. These two principles are required in order to obtain access into God's presence.

EXPERIENCING RADICAL WORSHIP:

This family worship experience will focus on receiving Jesus as your Lamb of God by taken communion together. Make sure you have led anyone into salvation that has not accepted it yet. End this time by offering up yourselves as living sacrifices to God in your worship.

Radical Worship
Family Devotional

The Bronze Laver

"Therefore we were buried with Him through baptism into death, that just as Christ was raised from the dead by the glory of the Father, even so we also should walk in newness of life." Romans 6:4

DAY 29

THE RESURRECTION OF CHRIST

The next step of worship through the tabernacle of Moses is the Bronze Laver. This furniture piece is also in the outer court of the tabernacle. The bronze laver was basically a very large bowl made out of bronze filled with water. The Priest would come over to the wash basin after sacrificing the animal and wash his hands and feet of the blood that had gotten on him during the sacrificial act of worship. This would make them clean and new again. The bible says that this act of worship was so important that if they did not do this step they would die when entering into the holy place (Exodus 30:21). The water of the Bronze Laver is a shadow of the Holy Spirit in which brought Jesus back to life (1 Peter 3:18). We experience Christ's death at the altar of sacrifice, but we experience His life at the bronze laver. The bronze laver represents the born again experience for us. In fact, when you were born in the natural you were held in your mothers belly by a sack of water, isn't it interesting that there is a bowl of water to represent the born again experience through Christ. Listen to the description of this act of worship in Titus 3:5-6, ***"according to His mercy He saved us, through the washing of regeneration and renewing of the Holy Spirit, ⁶ whom He poured out on us abundantly through Jesus Christ our Savior (NKJV).***

FAMILY DISCUSSION

As you read the above scriptures together discuss with your family the importance of not just receiving Jesus' death but His resurrection and life. Revisit the idea of being born again as we discussed in earlier devotions.

1. What was the Bronze Laver used for?
2. What does the water represent?
3. What does this act of worship represent to us?

Prayer: Jesus not only do we thank you for your death, we thank you for your life. It is because you were resurrected that we can be born again; you live in us through the Holy Spirit. Help us to never forget the victory of your resurrection. Amen.

DAY 30

WATER BAPTISM

According to scripture and in the order of the tabernacle, we understand that receiving Christ's death is the very first step of worship, the second step is receiving His life by the Holy Spirit, the third step is being water baptized as a testimony of what you have just done. Romans 6:3 says, **"When we are lowered into the water, it is like the burial of Jesus; when we are raised up out of the water, it is like the resurrection of Jesus" (MSG).** As the priest would wash with this water removing the stains of death it was as if they were water baptizing themselves as a testimony of Christ's death and resurrection. Water baptism allows us to testify publically that we (our flesh and own will) has been buried with Christ and now we live through Christ. When the priest would wash their hands, water now covered them. This water, which representing the Holy Spirit, was the very nature and character of Christ. Galatians 3:26-27 says it this way, **"Those who are baptized in the spirit put on Christ (NKJV).** At the bronze laver is where we choose to participate in the act of worship called water baptism; where we put on Christ. It is our declaration that we are going to become the hands and feet of Christ one earth. This last step of worship in the Outer Court prepares for the work of Christ in the Inner Court.

FAMILY DISCUSSION

During the discussion of this devotional take a bowl of water and demonstrate using fake blood or red paint what would happen at the Bronze laver.

1. Name the first three steps of God's order of worship?
2. What are we saying when we get water baptized?
3. What is it preparing us for?

Prayer: Jesus, let this family be a testimony of both your death and resurrection. Clothes us in you and prepare us to be your hands and feet. Amen.

Day 31

Baptism in the Spirit

It takes more than just to be covered in His spirit and looking like Him to do what he did on this earth. The bible says that we must have the mind of Christ. To think like and act like Jesus. Just as Jesus never did anything He didn't see or hear His father do, we are to do the same. How do we get the heart and mind of Christ?

As Jesus washed His disciples feet the night before He was crucified He said, **"If I then, your Lord and Teacher, have washed your feet, you also ought to wash one another's feet. ¹⁵ "For I have given you an example, that you should do as I have done to you" (John 13:14-16, NKJV).** Just as the water in the Laver represents the Holy Spirit the bronze bowl represents humanity; us in our flesh. God was foreshadowing for us at the bronze laver what He was going to do on the inside of us. As the disciples were instructed to wait in the upper room for the promise of the father, better known as the baptism of the Holy Spirit, before going to do the work of Jesus, we are to do the same. The power of the Holy Spirit filling you up, like the Bronze Laver filled up with water, is called the Baptism of the Holy Spirit. This fourth act of worship in the tabernacle of Moses gives you the power to think like and act like Jesus; this is where we receive the fruits and the gifts of the Spirit. Jesus said, **"He who believes in Me, as the Scripture has said, out of his heart will flow rivers of living water" (John 7:37-38, NKJV).**

Family Discussion

Revisit the story of Pentecost in Acts 2:21 and discuss the importance of the baptism of the Holy Spirit in preparation of doing the work of ministry with your family.

1. What is the fourth act of worship in the Tabernacle?
2. What does it help us do?
3. What does the bronze represent of the Laver?

Prayer: Jesus, we want all of you; not to be just clothed in you but to be filled with you by your Holy Spirit. Just like the disciples, we wait for the promise of the Father. Amen.

RADICAL WORSHIP
FAMILY REVIEW

"But now in Christ Jesus you who once were far off have been brought near by the blood of Christ."

Ephesians 2:13 (NKJV)

DAY 32

Your family should have the understanding through the last three lesson of what steps of worship it takes before entering into the inner court. The first step of worship at the Bronze Laver your family should have an understanding of is receiving the life of Christ. This step is so important because often times, as we worship, we stay at the death of Christ never entering into the life of Christ. The bronze laver visually gives us a picture of what it means to be born again. From there a natural transition will take place right into what water baptism is and means as the next step of worship. Your family lastly should have an understanding as to the last step of worship at the bronze laver; the baptism of the Holy Spirit.

EXPERIENCING RADICAL WORSHIP:

Your family worship time today will be all about receiving His life at the bronze laver. Take the bowl of water that you used during the devotion and wash everyone's hands and pray over them to receive Christ's life. You may also want to have a water baptism service at your home in a bath tub or swimming pool or make arrangements with your Pastor to do it at church. At the end of this worship time concentrate on the baptism of the Holy Spirit, make sure to pray for anyone who has not received yet.

RADICAL WORSHIP
FAMILY DEVOTIONAL

THE LAMPSTAND

*"The spirit of a man is the lamp of the LORD,
Searching all the inner depths of his heart."*

Proverbs 20:27

DAY 33

THE LIGHT THAT BRINGS REPENTANCE

We are going to move from the outer court into the inner court of the tabernacle of Moses. This room focuses on the Holy Spirit of the Trinity and is about the work of ministry in us and through us. This Jewish menorah is a smaller version of what you would have seen as the Lampstand in the Tabernacle. It was basically the lamp that lit the entire inner court of the tabernacle. But instead of it being powered by electricity or candle wax, it was powered by oil. As we talked about it in a previous devotional the oil represents Holy Spirit. The Holy Spirit has many jobs on this earth. One of the jobs of the Holy Spirit is foreshadowed at the Lampstand; to uncover the hidden things of our hearts. Proverbs 20:27 says, *"The spirit of a man is the lamp of the LORD, Searching all the inner depths of his heart" (NKJV).* This is what David was asking for in Psalms 139:23 when he asked God to search him. The Holy Spirit comes into our hearts with His light, the truth of God, and shines it into the dark places of our soul revealing to us sin and thoughts that are not of God. Why is this act of worship important? So that we may repent, change the way we think, into the mind of Christ. This act of worship that leads us to repentance must be done in order for us to be in the presence of God's holiness and to become like His son Jesus.

FAMILY DISCUSSION

Pull up a picture of the Inner Court, Lampstand of the Tabernacle, as well as a Jewish Menorah to give more of an understanding as to what it looked like. Use a flashlight in a dark room as an object lesson to demonstrate how light reveals things hidden in the dark.

1. What does the Oil in the Lampstand represent?
2. What does the light of the Holy Spirit in us do?
3. Why is repentance so important for us?

Prayer: Holy Spirit we invite you now to search the hidden places of the heart of each of us in this family; brings us to a place of conviction and repentance that we may become more like Christ. Amen.

DAY 34

THE LIGHT THAT BRINGS REVELATION

The second foreshadow of the lampstand in us is the Holy Spirit bringing us into revelation of who God is and what His word means. Revelation means to be brought into more of a full understanding of something that you previously knew a little about. Many religious leaders and Israelites of Jesus' day saw Jesus; they heard Him speak, they saw Him perform miracles, but they did not have a revelation of who Jesus truly was; they only saw Jesus in part. But Jesus asked Peter **"But who do you say that I am?" [16] Simon Peter answered and said, "You are the Christ, the Son of the living God." [17] Jesus answered and said to him, "Blessed are you, Simon Bar-Jonah, for flesh and blood has not revealed this to you, but My Father who is in heaven" (Matt 16:15-18, NKJV).** The Spirit of God had revealed who Jesus was to Peter. The light of the Holy Spirit illuminates hidden things within God's word and Kingdom to reveal to us deeper revelation of who He is and who we are to Him. The bible calls these hidden things mysteries. Jesus says in Luke 8:10 that as children of God, the Holy Spirit will reveal to us the mysteries of God and His kingdom. When we worship God at the lampstand we are allowing the light of the Holy Spirit to reveal mysteries in God's Kingdom.

FAMILY DISCUSSION

Take a flashlight and shine it on your bible demonstrating that there are hidden things in the word and in God's kingdom. The Holy Spirit in us, if we allow Him to, will reveal some of them to us. Look up and discuss Luke 8:10 together.

1. What does revelation mean?
2. What did Peter have that the religious leaders did not have?
3. Who gives us revelation of God's word, who He is, and of His kingdom?

Prayer: Holy Spirit we desire to have deeper revelation of who God is and what His kingdom is all about. Come; allow your light to shine in us revealing the mysteries of the kingdom. Amen.

DAY 35

BEING THE LIGHT

Remember the inner court room is not only about the work of the Holy Spirit in us, but it is about the work of the Holy Spirit through us. *"You are the light of the world. A city that is set on a hill cannot be hidden. ¹⁵ "Nor do they light a lamp and put it under a basket, but on a lampstand, and it gives light to all who are in the house. ¹⁶ "Let your light so shine before men, that they may see your good works and glorify your Father in heaven (Matt 5:14-16, NKJV).* These are the words of Jesus to us. Isn't it interesting that he would use the very word lampstand in this scripture as he tells us that we are the light to the world? So how do we become the light to the world? Jesus tells us in this very scripture, *"that they may see your good works".* The last act of worship at the lampstand of the tabernacle is to go and do for others. The light of the Holy Spirit on the inside of us, changes us into the nature and character of Jesus. He then gives us the very power we need to share that light with others around us. We share our light within us by what we do and say to our neighbors, our friends, and our family. We let the lampstand within us shine for others to see until they can't help but to repent and gain a deeper revelation of God by the Holy Spirit.

FAMILY DISCUSSION

Discuss some ways with your family you can shine your light on each other and others you know around you. As your family members demonstrate some of these things to each other, have them shine a flashlight on each other.

1. What does the Lampstand in us become for others to see?
2. When others see our good works through the Holy Spirit what happens to them?
3. What is it called when we shine our light for others to see?

Prayer: Holy Spirit we desire to be a family who allows our good works through the Holy Spirit to shine for others to see. Help us to shine our light for others that we may reach the lost for you. Amen.

RADICAL WORSHIP
FAMILY REVIEW

*"The spirit of a man is the lamp of the LORD,
Searching all the inner depths of his heart"*

Proverbs 20:27 (NKJV)

DAY 36

In the last three devotionals your family should have gained an understanding that the light of the Holy Spirit reveals to us our sin and ungodly thoughts hidden in the places of our soul. This process leads us to engage in the act of worship called repentance. The second foreshadow revealed to us at the lampstand is the working light of the Holy Spirit in us to bring greater revelation of who God is and who He is within us. The third foreshadow that is revealed at the lampstand that your family should have an understanding of is the act of worship called evangelism. This is the place where we allow the light of the Holy Spirit within us to shine brightly for others to see as we serve others through our good works.

EXPERIENCING RADICAL WORSHIP:

Your family worship experience will focus on all three aspects of the lampstand. You will first encourage the Holy Spirit to begin to shine into the dark places of their hearts bringing them to repentance for things which are revealed. After this time of reflection and repentance, have the family stand, sit, or lay down as they soak in God's presence allowing Him to reveal mysteries of His Kingdom to them. Lastly pray one for another allowing the Holy Spirit to shine His light through each one. Challenge your family to take time to serve a friend or neighbor this week.

Radical Worship
Family Devotional

The Table of Showbread

"Man shall not live by bread alone, but by every word that proceeds from the mouth of God." Matthew 4:4

DAY 37

COLLECTING THE BREAD

From the Lampstand, directly across the room is called the Table of Showbread. It was simply a table that the priest would display the bread and grain offerings on from the people (exodus 25:23). To begin to explore the foreshadows revealed at this table we must look at a story in the bible found in Exodus 16. The Israelites were stuck in the wilderness, tired and hungry. They had already forgotten the promise of God to bring them into a land filled with milk and honey. So the bible says that God heard their complaints and rained down bread from heaven for them to eat everyday. Exodus 16:31 says it was like coriander seed and tasted like honey. The interesting thing about this seed is that it is white like milk and it tasted like honey which sounds a lot like their promise from God to be given a land filled with milk and honey(Exodus 3:8). So, at first glance we can see how the bread on the table of showbread spiritually was a reminder of the promises of God. Today we don't have bread raining down from heaven, but what we do have to eat to remind us of the promises of God, is the word of God. God instructed the Israelites to collect this bread daily; not just once a week or in church. In fact if they tried to skip a day and eat off of yesterday's bread it would get moldy. We must be reminded of God's promises for us every day.

FAMILY DISCUSSION

Pull up a picture of the Table of Showbread and coriander seed on the internet. As your read the above scriptures together, discuss how you can make sure to read your bible everyday so that you do not lose sight of God's promises.

1. What was the bread from heaven like?
2. What did the bread from heaven represent to God?
3. How often did they have to collect and eat this bread?

Prayer: God through this devotional you have taught our family that reading the word of God is an act of worship you desire of us. Help us to take the time to do that and help us be reminded daily by your word your promises to this family. Amen.

DAY 38

EATING THE BREAD

The bread was not just collected it was ate. Jesus said when rebuking the devil in the wilderness, *"Man shall not live by bread alone, but by every word that proceeds from the mouth of God" (Matt 4:4, NKJV).* Our natural bodies need food to eat, but spiritually we need God's word just as much. Our spirits will die without constantly being nourished by God's word. God beckons us to, *"Taste and see that the Lord is good, Blessed be the man who trusts in Him (Psalms 34:8, NKJV).* God is asking us to eat His word and see if it is not good...we must trust Him. God commanded Ezekiel to eat the scroll of God, God's word, so that he would not just collect God's word, but that it would become a part of him (Ezekiel 3:1). You see it is easy to read the bible and memorize a scripture or two, but unless you get the words of God inside of you it will never be a part of who you are; you will not ever believe it. God says in Isaiah 55:10 that His word is like seed that is planted and produces the fruit that he said it was going to. When we eat God's word it becomes not just something we know, but something we GROW. Mixing what we read with the presence of the Spirit enables the Holy Spirit to take it from our minds to our spirits. This makes that old phrase "You are what you eat" true in our lives!

FAMILY DISCUSSION

Discuss with your family the difference between memorizing a scripture and knowing it in your spirit. Have your family eat matza bread as you read scriptures as a good object lesson. Discuss situation where the word of good produce good fruit in your lives.

1. Why does the Lord want us to eat the bread (word)?
2. What is the difference between memorizing the word and knowing the word?
3. How do we eat the word of God?

Prayer: God may we eat your word each and every day. Let us not just know your word but grow your word deep within our spirits. We trust you and believe that what you said you would do you will do in this family. Amen.

DAY 39

SPEAKING THE PROMISE

Does anyone know what God's problem was with the Israelites in the wilderness? They complained too much. Even though they knew what God had really done for them they spoke something very different. They choose to speak the opposite of what they just had eaten. They should have been saying how good God is, how sweet he is, instead they complained for forty years in the wilderness and most died before ever seeing the promise land. The bible says in Proverbs 18:21, **"Death and life are in the power of the tongue, And those who love it will eat its fruit" (NKJV).** This means that whatever we say has the power to produce that in our lives or other people lives. God has given us His promises, He desires us to eat them, and then lastly we must speak them into existence. If I simply plant this seed in soil will it grow into a sunflower? You must give the seed water and sunlight. When we mix reading God's word with the spirit we water the seed, but when we begin to speak it we release it into the light of Jesus allowing full growth of the promise of God on the inside of us to produce its fruit. Psalms 71:24 says, **"My tongue also shall talk of Your righteousness all the day long" (NKJV).** Speaking, praying, and singing the word of God is the last step of worship at the Table of Showbread; we do this for ourselves and in ministry to others.

FAMILY DISCUSSION

Take time to teach your family how to pray/sing God's word back to God. Use scriptures from the last three days to do this together. You can also plant some fruit plants together to remind yourself of God's promises (seed) on the inside of you.

1. Why did the Israelites wonder in the wilderness for forty years?
2. The power of what and what is in our tongues?
3. What happens when we speak, pray, or sing God's word back to Him?

Prayer: God help us to guard our mouths that what we speak is life and not death. May we speak according to your word no matter the circumstances. I pray now send your word forth from our mouths and produce your fruit in this family. Amen.

RADICAL WORSHIP
FAMILY REVIEW

*"The spirit of a man is the lamp of the LORD,
Searching all the inner depths of his heart"*

Proverbs 20:27 (NKJV)

DAY 40

In the last three days your family should have gained an understanding of the importance of God's word; how to read it, believe it, and speak it into existence for themselves and others. Through the story in Exodus when God rained down Manna from heaven for the Israelites, clues unfold for us that reveal the foreshadowing of what this place in the tabernacle is all about; the promises of God through His word. Your family should be able to see how the Israelites collecting the bread daily for food is a picture for how we are to read God's word daily. The second foreshadow is that we are not to just memorize the word but to eat the word getting it inside our spirit that it may become a part of who we are. The last foreshadow revealed the step of worship that the Israelites neglected to do that kept them wondering in the dessert for forty years; speaking, praying, and singing the word of God.

EXPERIENCING RADICAL WORSHIP:

Your family worship time today will obviously focus on the word of God and how your family can use it to minister to themselves and others. Have a list of promise scriptures ready that your family can look up and read as they soak in the presence of God. Than end your worship time by declaring the scriptures you just read over each other.

Radical Worship
Family Devotional

The Altar of Incense

"And walk in love, as Christ also has loved us and given Himself for us, an offering and a sacrifice to God for a sweet-smelling aroma." Ephesians 5:2

Day 41

The Scent of Our Worship

The last step of worship before entering into Inner Most Court is the Altar of Incense. The Altar of Incense is where the priest was required to burn incense day and night (Exodus 30:7-8). Incense is a piece of wood that has many different kinds of oils on it that gives off a good sent. Ephesians 5:2 tells us, *"walk in love, as Christ also has loved us and given Himself for us, an offering and a sacrifice to God for a sweet-smelling aroma" (NKJV).* When we express God's love that is worship, and that worship has the power to create and smell. A scent of something can make you feel good or it can make you feel bad. Our worship has the same power with God. God said in Isaiah1:13, *"Bring no more futile sacrifices; Incense is an abomination to Me" (NKJV).* Worship that does not come from the heart is foul smelling to God. Luke 10:27 says, *"You shall love the LORD your God with all your heart, with all your soul, with all your strength, and with all your mind and 'your neighbor as yourself" (NKJV).* Our worship to God must be to give all of our self, that is why this is called an altar; a sacrifice unto the Lord. The incense was to burned continually, that is a picture of how we are to have a lifestyle of worship unto God.

Family Discussion

Take time with your family to smell many different scents (good and bad) from your kitchen expressing how they make you feel. As you pull a picture of incense up on the internet or purchase real incense to use, discuss ways you can bring a bad scent and a good sweet smelling aroma to God through your worship.

1. What is the Altar of Incense a foreshadow of?
2. When we don't give all our heart in worship what does it produce?
3. Why is this place called an altar?

Prayer: God help us by your grace and spirit to give you all our worship. May our offering of worship be always a sweet smelling aroma to you. Amen.

Day 42

The Cloud of God's Presence

As incense was burned a cloud of smoke would bellow out from it. This smoke is a foreshadowing of God's presence. God said to the Israelites, *"And the LORD went before them by day in a pillar of cloud to lead the way".* James 4:8 says that as we draw near to God He draws near to us. This means as we worship it produces God presence; the Holy Spirit. As we lift up our hands, sing praises to Him, as we share God's love with others, as we obey His word, His presence comes down and lifts our worship up to God. The scent of our worship is mixed with the cloud of His presence and is offered up before God. We don't see clouds as evidence of God's presence today like the Israelites did in the wilderness. However we can see, feel, and even hear the evidence of the presence of God in our lives in many ways. The first way is by feeling and giving love. God is love so it is impossible to feel love or give love without his presence. Some people describe feeling God's love as if a warm blanket was wrapped around them, as rushing water covering them, or rushing wind, or through peace, joy, power, gifts of the spirit, and many more because these are the very characteristics of the Holy Spirit.

Family Discussion

It will be very helpful if you have real incense to demonstrate the smoke with. Discuss with your families each have experience the cloud of God's presence as they worshiped.

1. What is the smoke of the incense a foreshadowing of?
2. How do we produce the smoke of God's presence in our lives?
3. What are some ways that you can feel, see, and hear God's presence?

Prayer: God help us to see, feel, and hear your presence produced in our life as we worship you. As we draw near to you, draw near to us and touch us with your presence. Amen.

DAY 43

LOVING OTHERS THROUGH OUR WORSHIP

The last we are going to explore at the Altar of Incense is how we serve others at this place of worship. We mentioned earlier Luke 10:27, **"You shall love the LORD your God with all your heart, with all your soul, with all your strength, and with all your mind,' and 'your neighbor as yourself" (NKJV).** Not only does this scripture tell us to love God with all that we are, but it tells us that we must love others. Worship is not only expressing our love to God, it is expressing God's love to others. Psalms 141:2 says, **"Let my prayer be set before You as incense, The lifting up of my hands as the evening sacrifice" (Psalms 141:2, NKJV).** The Altar of Incense is where we get to worship God through intercession; prayers for others. Intercession simply is when we stand between a person and heaven and pray for them; it is also called standing in the gap for someone. Just as our praise goes up before God through the smoke/cloud of His presence so do our prayers. In fact, the most effective prayers we can pray is in the midst of worship and the presence of God, because it is through the spirit we can pray God's will for someone. In revelation 8:3-5 it says that your prayers is captured by the angels and presented before God, and when the time comes to answer that prayer, it is thrown to the earth with thunder and lightning.

FAMILY DISCUSSION

Look up and read revelations 8:3-5 together as you discuss the truth about our prayers mixed with our worship rising to God. Once again if you have incense, lite them, to demonstrate this truth.

1. What is one way we can express our love for others at the Altar of Incense?
2. What is intercession?
3. What happens to our prayers?

Prayer: God, give us a heart of intercession in this home. As we worship, bring your heart through your Holy Spirit that we may pray how and what you desire us to pray for others. Amen.

RADICAL WORSHIP
FAMILY REVIEW

*"The spirit of a man is the lamp of the LORD,
Searching all the inner depths of his heart"*

Proverbs 20:27 (NKJV)

DAY 44

Through the last three days devotional your family should gain an understanding of how their worship affects God, what it produces in their life, and how to worship God through interceding for others effectively. Your family through the foreshadowing of the incense will be able to literally smell how their worship affects God. They will be encouraged to worship God with all of themselves, knowing that if they don't, they run the risk of smelling sticky to God. Moving forward your family should have an understanding of how their worship produces the cloud of God's presence. Lastly, each member of your family should now understand how they can use the presence of God produced in their worship to most effectively pray for others.

EXPERIENCING RADICAL WORSHIP:

Your family worship time will be centered around worshipping God with your whole heart producing a sweet smelling aroma. Encourage them to become aware of the cloud of God's presence being produced. End the time by having praying one for another.

RADICAL WORSHIP
FAMILY DEVOTIONAL

THE ARK OF THE COVENANT

"He who dwells in the secret place of the Most High Shall abide under the shadow of the Almighty." Psalms 91:1

DAY 45

THE FULLNESS OF GOD'S PRESENCE

Now we are ready to step into the room we have been waiting for, the Inner Most court, the Most Holy place, where the Ark of the Covenant or the ark of testimony, is. In this room, inside the box of the ark was were the holy presence of God was contained. The high priest of Moses' day was only able to come into this room, separated by a veil, once a year where he was commanded to bring in the blood of a sacrifice and incense from the altar of worship (Leviticus 16:11-14). Today as priests unto God, our spirits have become the very dwelling place of God, meaning we have become that room and ark, twenty four-seven. The bible says **"Therefore, brethren, having boldness to enter the Holiest by the blood of Jesus, [20] by a new and living way which He consecrated for us, through the veil, that is, His flesh" (Hebrew 10:19-20, NKJV).** Today there is still a veil we must go through; the blood of the Lamb of God that we received at the altar of sacrifice. And guess what, we still need the incense which produces the Holy Spirit found at the altar of our worship. There are no shortcuts to get to God, but when we finally step into that room both Father (within the Ark), Son (The blood of Jesus we received at the Altar of Sacrifice), and Holy Spirit (represented through the Altar of Incense) are represented; the fullness of who God is. It is through Jesus and our worship that we get to be in the presence of a Holy God.

FAMILY DISCUSSION

Pull up a picture of the Ark of the Covenant on the internet and discuss the idea that we are that place that holds God's presence now.

1. What is one way we can express our love for others at the Altar of Incense?
2. What is intercession?
3. What happens to our prayers?

Prayer: God, thank you that you have made us your home. We are your tabernacle and through the blood of Jesus and our sacrifice of worship we can dwell in your Holy Presence. We want your fullness, nothing missing or lacking. Amen.

DAY 46

THE POWER OF GOD'S PRESENCE

In the Most Holy place is where we do nothing and God does everything. In the outer and inner court something was required of us, but once we step into this room God does all the work and we simply receive. In 1 Kings 8:11 this is what happened to the priest as the cloud of God's glory filled the tent. In exodus 24:17 it says, ***"The sight of the glory of the LORD was like a consuming fire" (Exodus, 24:17, NKJV).*** Remember, the very glory of God, His holiness and righteousness, is what lights up the room of the most holy place. This light of holiness was a fire that would burn out anything not holy that it touches. This all-consuming fire of God is also used to burn up our enemies (Deuteronomy 9:3). This doesn't mean that God will literally burn up people who don't like you, but it does mean that as you stand still in His presence you allow God to fight your battles for you. These truths should lead us to have a holy fear of God, but a fear of reverence and respect for who God is and the power He holds in our lives. As long as we come to God under the blood of His son we will not physically die, but our sin dies. The more we step into the most holy place with God, the more we become holy, sanctified, and safe from our enemies; the consuming fire of God's holiness burns away our sin and our enemies. This understanding and honor to who God is and what He can do is called the fear of the Lord.

FAMILY DISCUSSION

Pull up the scriptures reference in the above teaching and discuss them with your family. Make sure they understand what it means to fear God as they worship in His presence.

1. What do we do in the Most Holy Place?
2. What lights up this room?
3. What does God's glory have the power to do?

Prayer: God, we ask for your glory in this family. We ask that you send your power to burn up the sin of our enemies and our sin that we may become holy as you are holy. Amen.

DAY 47

THE LIFE'S IN GOD'S PRESENCE

It is thought that the glory of the Lord rests in between the wings of the angels on top of the Ark of the Covenant. As His glory shined it would cast a shadow off the angels. This gives us a clear picture as to what Psalms 91:1 means when it says, *"He who dwells in the secret place of the Most High shall abide under the shadow of the Almighty" (NKJV).* We abide, which means to rest or be with, right in God's glory under the wings. Who has ever felt like hiding, perhaps from people who make fun of you, distractions that keep you from God, just from a rough day? In psalms 16:11 it says we find joy and pleasure in His presence. We also feel His love for God is love. We also find life in His presence. In the Old Testament, Aarons' rod, which is in the ark of the covenant, was actually a dead almond branch and as it laid in God's glory in the most holy place it began to bud and came back to life. In Malachi 4:2 says we find healing in His wings. Lastly, it is the place were God speaks to you, *"There I will meet with you, and I will speak with you from above the mercy seat, from between the two cherubim which are on the ark of the testimony" (Exodus 25:22, NKJV).* God desires to not just be with His children, He desires to speak to His children. It is really hard to hear what someone is saying when you're the one doing the ministering, the praying, and the work; in the place of God's glory we become still and listen for God to speak to us.

FAMILY DISCUSSION

Pull up the scriptures reference in the above teaching and discuss them with your family. Show them a picture of the wings that would cast the shadow.

1. Where do we dwell with God?
2. Name three things we find in the shadow of God's presence?
3. What does God do in this place of worship?

Prayer: God, hide this family in the shadow of your wings. May we find rest, your peace, your joy and love in the most Holy place. Speak to us God as we are still and listen. Amen.

RADICAL WORSHIP
FAMILY REVIEW

*"The spirit of a man is the lamp of the LORD,
Searching all the inner depths of his heart"*

Proverbs 20:27 (NKJV)

DAY 48

The last three devotional should have brought your family into an understanding of the prerequisite to get into God's presence; there are no shortcuts and there are requirements before entering the most holy place. This will than give them a beautiful picture of how the fullness of God (Father, Son, and Holy Spirit), is experienced at the ark of Covenant.

After establishing how to enter into the most holy place and what the ark represents, your family should have gained an understanding that this is the only place along the road of the tabernacle that they do nothing and God does it all. They should have learned that this is the place that their sin burns in the glory of God's holiness and God's holiness is a mighty power that burns their enemies. Lastly your family should have learned that God hides them in the shadow of the most high and gives them rest, joy, love, life, and most of all this is the very place we go to be still and hear God's voice.

EXPERIENCING RADICAL WORSHIP:

Your family worship time today will be centered around the most holy place and the ark of the covenant. Invite your family to find a place to lie down as they begin to rest in the presence of the Lord. Encourage them to listen for God's voice and allow God to minister to their hearts as they need Him to.

RADICAL WORSHIP
FAMILY DEVOTIONAL

RADICAL WORSHIP

"Do you see this woman? I entered your house; you gave Me no water for My feet, but she has washed My feet with her tears and wiped them with the hair of her head. [45] "You gave Me no kiss, but this woman has not ceased to kiss My feet since the time I came in. [46] "You did not anoint My head with oil, but this woman has anointed My feet with fragrant oil. [47] "Therefore I say to you, her sins, which are many, are forgiven, for she loved much." Luke 7:44-47

DAY 49

FROM THE LAW TO THE HEART

Who remembers the story of Mary and her expensive perfume poured out on Jesus? She wanted to worship Jesus so much that she took the most expensive thing she had, her favorite perfume, and she poured it on Jesus' head and cried at His feet, washing His feet with her tears and hair (Luke 7:37-38). She loved Jesus enough to give him all she had, plus herself, too. The disciples didn't understand this kind of worship yet, and were upset at Jesus for letting her do that. But Jesus said to them that because she had given all she had to worship Him **"Wherever this gospel is preached in the whole world, what this woman has done will also be told as a memorial to her" (Mark 14:9, NKJV).** The disciples and the Jewish people had only been taught to worship God from the law not their hearts. Jesus used the law of God to foreshadow the heart of worship in this story. When the disciples began to question this women's way of worship, Jesus rebukes them and honors her for her love towards Him (Luke 7:44-47). You see it was a law of God for an Israelite to honor a man who enters His house by giving him water to wash his feet or washing his feet for him, by greeting him with a kiss, and by blessing him and his household. All three of these things she did to honor and worship Jesus, but not by the law but from the heart of her worship. She did what was required to honor someone who comes into your home, so should we as Jesus comes into our home or tabernacle.

FAMILY DISCUSSION

Pull up the story of Mary found in Luke 7:37-38. Discuss with your family Jesus' response to Mary's worship and how it perfectly reflects how we are to honor Jesus in our worship.

1. What did Mary use to anoint Jesus and wash His feet?
2. What three things did Mary fulfill according to the law with her heart of worship?
3. Why is what she did so important to Jesus?

Prayer: May our life, and all we are and have as a family, be poured upon you like an alabaster box Jesus. May we honor you as you come into our house, our heart, to live. Amen.

DAY 50

MARY'S TABERNACLE WORSHIP

Mary's act of worship would be the dots to connect the Old Testament of Worship through the law to the New Testament of worship through the heart, just like the gospel would connect the dots between the Old Covenant of God and the New Covenant of God through Christ. Mary visited every furniture piece of the blueprints of worship found in the Tabernacle of Worship. Jesus said that she was preparing Him for His death, at Jesus's feet she was at the altar of sacrifice. As she broke open that expensive perfume bottle called an alabaster box, she poured all that she had and herself on the altar of sacrifice for Jesus. She then stepped right over to the bronze Laver as she began to wash Jesus' feet with her tears (water). She was washing the death of the earth and this world from Jesus. Next, she stepped right into the inner court at the lampstand as she anointed Jesus' head with oil. Stepping right over to the table of showbread we can see how she honored the word of God by performing all three laws of honoring someone who has come into your house. We then see a shadow of the altar of incense as her worship produced a sweet smelling aroma as she broke open that alabaster box. Lastly, she steps right into the most holy place at the Ark of the Covenant as she then hears the voice of Jesus tell her that she is cleansed and forgiven.

FAMILY DISCUSSION

Make sure to have pictures of the Tabernacle and all its furniture pieces. Have your family try to guess how her worship demonstrated each step of the Tabernacle.

1. What did Mary's worship connect the dots to?
2. Name three furniture pieces and how she demonstrated worship at each one.
3. What happened last to Mary in this story?

Prayer: Jesus lets us take Mary's worship experience and use it as a example in our own worship. May we move you like Mary moved you. Amen.

DAY 51

RADICAL WORSHIPPERS

Jesus took Mary's heart of worship and set the scene for how we can take God's blueprints and apply them to the tabernacle of our own hearts. By her very act of worship she changed the way traditional worship was done and at the same time causes us to go back to the roots of why worship was established to begin with. This is the very definition of radical; an extreme difference of what is traditionally the case coupled with forming a basis, foundation, and going to the root of something. She is the definition of a radical worshipper. Today Jesus desires us to become that same radical worshipper as well; to worship Him with our whole heart and soul and mind, not because of the law, but through the law from our hearts. We are to be expressive and sacrificial with our worship, not holding anything back—just like Mary; to be a living sacrifice of worship (Romans 12:1). The most important gift we have to pour onto Jesus is ourselves. Mary did not care what those disciples thought about her, and we must not care either. Jesus bragged about this woman for worshipping with all her heart and soul, if Jesus brags about you that should be all that matters. Like Mary, your radical worship will be used by Jesus to bring others into this radical lifestyle of worship and to bring others back to the heart of what and why we worship.

FAMILY DISCUSSION

Discuss with your family the calling into radical worship and what it means to be a radical worshipper. Discuss with them some of things Mary had to go through, like persecution, and how they will have to go through the same thing as a radical worshipper.

1. What two things did Mary do to the culture of worship in her time through worship?
2. Should we care what others think about our worship?
3. How will God use our radical worship?

Prayer: We declare that this family will be radical worshippers. That like Mary, we will not hold anything back, but worship with our whole heart, soul, and body. Use us to change the culture of worship in our day. Amen.

RADICAL WORSHIP
FAMILY REVIEW

*"The spirit of a man is the lamp of the LORD,
Searching all the inner depths of his heart"*

Proverbs 20:27 (NKJV)

DAY 52

Through the last three days your family should be able to connect the dots between the Old Testament worship at the tabernacle of Moses through the law and the New Testament worship by the spirit through the heart of each believer. Through Mary's act of worship a beautiful picture unfolds on how we can translate Tabernacle Worship into worship in the spirit and through the heart. Your family should have gained an understanding how Mary followed the law of how each Israelite was to honor a person who came into their home; except she did it through her heart and not by tradition. Each family member should see a the shadow unfold of how we are to honor Jesus as he steps into our home within our own heart, they should have a clear picture that true worship carries the same principles as the laws of God, but through the heart of flesh. Secondly your family should have gained an understanding as to how Mary visited literally every furniture piece of the tabernacle. Lastly, through Mary's worship, radical worship is now defined to your family with prayer that each heart is stirred to become a radical worshipper.

EXPERIENCING RADICAL WORSHIP:

Your family worship time will bring everything together that you have learned in each section of this devotional. You will take your family on a journey leading them to one furniture piece at a time, stopping at each one to spend time in specific worship which defines each step in the blueprints of God. I have made a diagram on the next page with suggested acts of worship for your family.

FAMILY ACTS OF WORSHIP THROUGH THE TABERNACLE

Have each person lie down and just rest in the Presence of God as they listen for His voice and open their eyes to see inside the Spirit.

Spend a few minutes first in deep worship. Than have each person begin to intercede in prayer over situations or others in their life.

Lite several candles in a dark room and spend time asking the Holy Spirit to bring you to repentance of anything hidden in their heart.

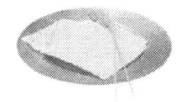

Have scriptures for each person to read out loud. Than together have everyone repeat the scripture as a prayer.

Either a home/church water baptism or have each person wash their hands in the Bronze laver.

Take Communion, leaving room for anyone that needs to receive Christ to do so.

Start Here

Family Resources Recommended

Presence-Driven Family Worship For Your Home
I highly recommended purchasing this resource for your families within your church to read as you begin to birth presence-driven family ministry. This will help them grab hold of the vision for their families and inspire them to engage in your ministry and in home family worship.

Stone Moments Family Manual
Although written for families, I highly recommended purchasing this resource as you begin hosting family gatherings. It has 72 creative spirit lead acts of worship you can do with your families.

Act of Worship
This resource although written as a church curriculum, is an excellent resource for home. All 52 acts of worship in this curriculum are in the Stone Moments Manual but in this resource each one comes with a full teaching for your families. This resource covers the acts of worship from simply raising of your hands, knelling, clapping, and singing, to more of the deeper worship like praying in the spirit and listening for the voice of God.

Radical Worship Family Devotional
Your families will go on a 52 day journey of worship from before the earth was created, to the Garden of Eden, through the Tabernacle of Moses, to the Garden of Gethsemane with Jesus, right to Mary's alabaster box. The Tabernacle teaching in this book came straight out of the pages of this devotional to be shared as a family with discussion questions and presence-driven family worship exercises.

Living Stones Family Devotional

Through a detailed word study of how God has chosen to use stones in the "seen" world, a picture begins to form that reveals who we are as living stones in the "unseen" world according to 1 Peter 2:4. Your families will take a 40 day journey from the Old Testament to the New, discovering mysteries hidden in God's word to find your calling as Living Stones. This devotional is filled with creative spirit lead worship activities that go along with each subject learned.

Kingdom Family Devotional

This resource is full of 84 days your families can experience learning about our King and the Kingdom of Heaven together. Through the view finder of a kingdom, they will discover their own purpose for being born on this earth and feel a since of belonging to something greater than themselves. Spirit filled acts of worship is all included in this resources for your families as it pertains to the subject.

Amazing Grace Family Devotional

This 52 day devotional is all about helping your families find Biblical authentic grace. This resource brings a holistic view of grace that encompasses a foundation of grace based upon a biblical perspective of who God is, who we are not, why we need grace through Christ, the right posture to receive grace, and what the work of grace produces in every believer and family that is yielded to the Holy Spirit. There are opportunities given for presence-driven family worship in the devotional as well.

Made in United States
Troutdale, OR
09/02/2023